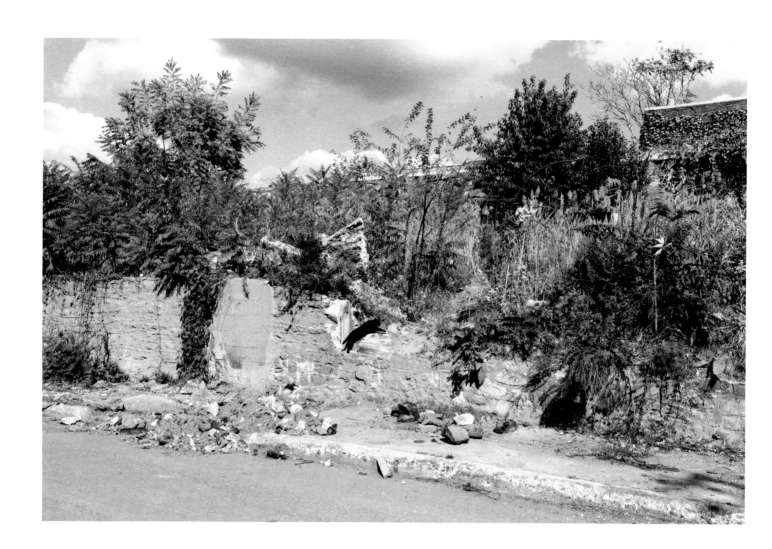

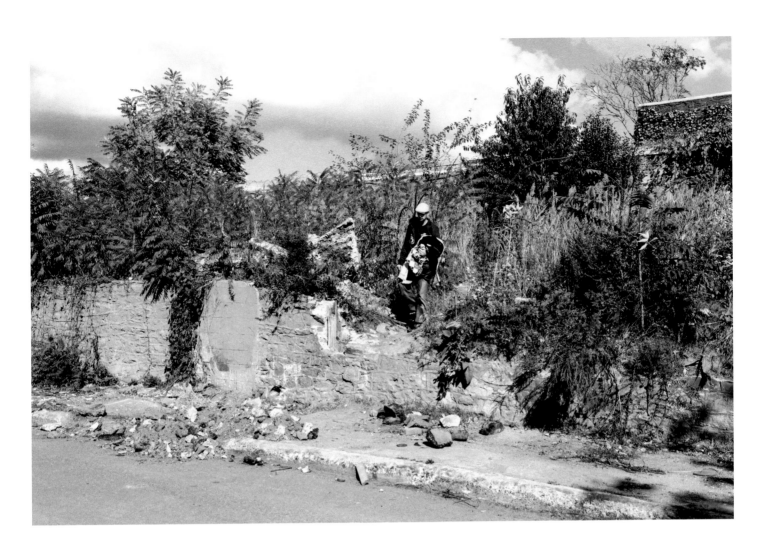

GOOD

JORDAN BAUMGARTEN

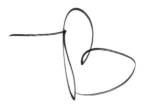

SICK

GOST

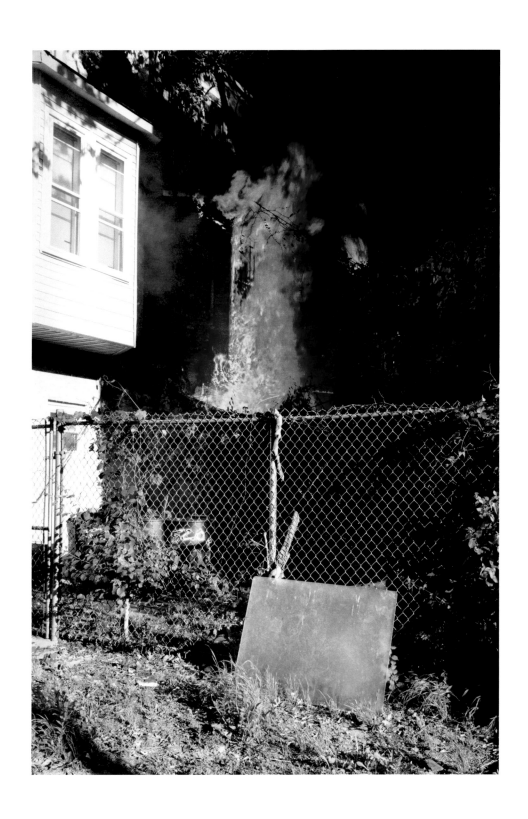

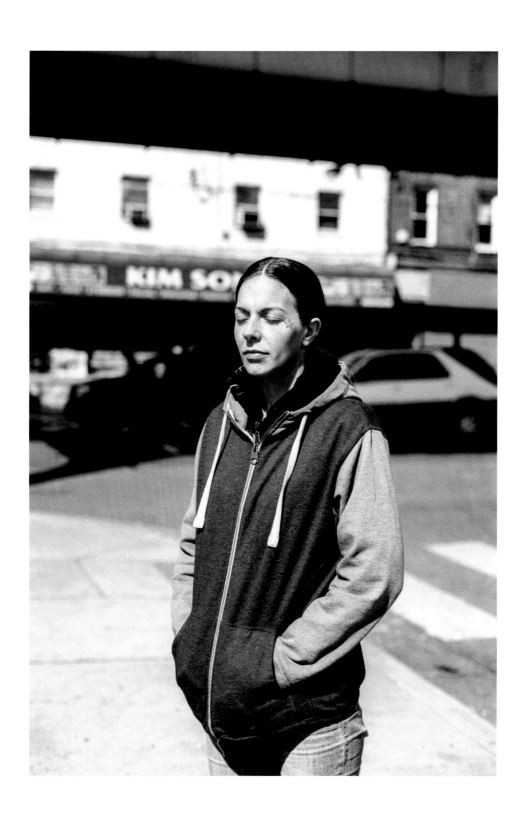

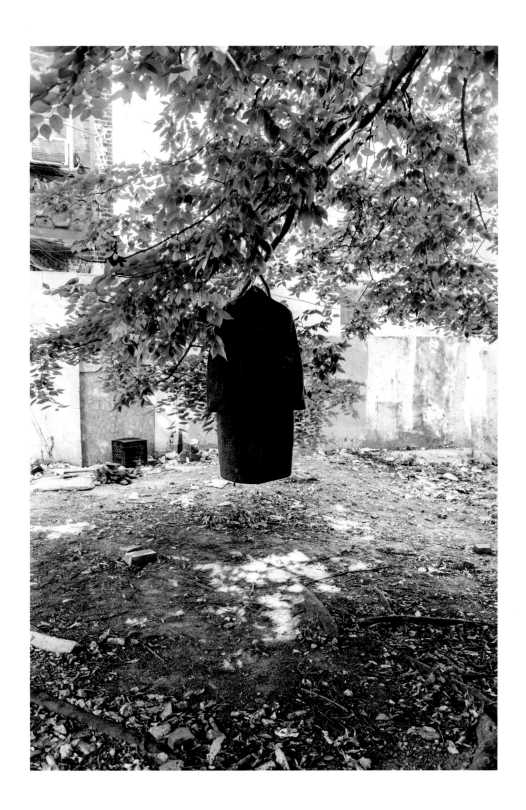

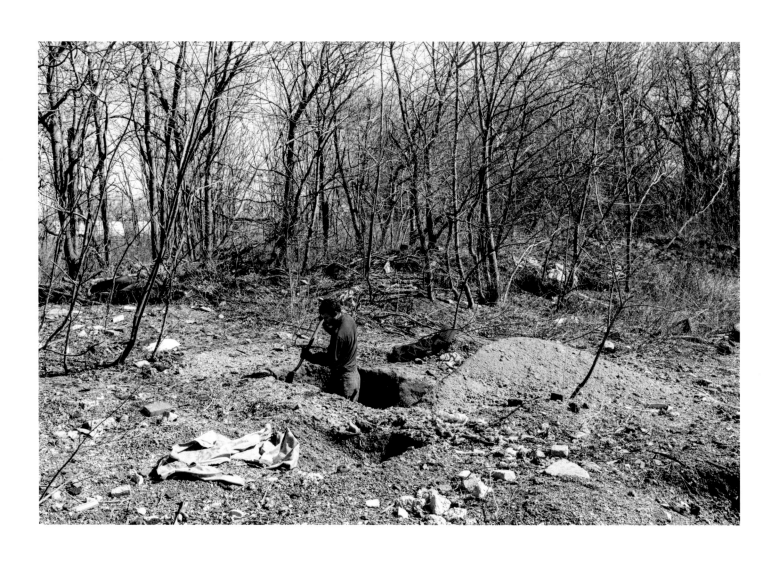

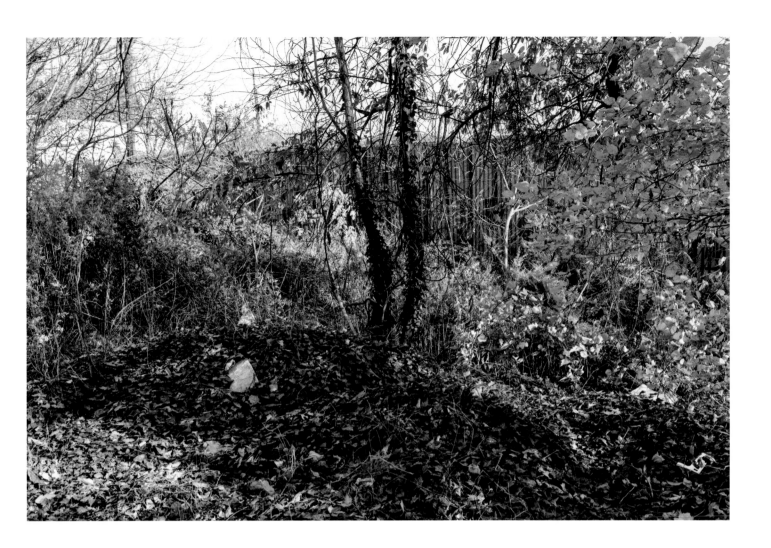

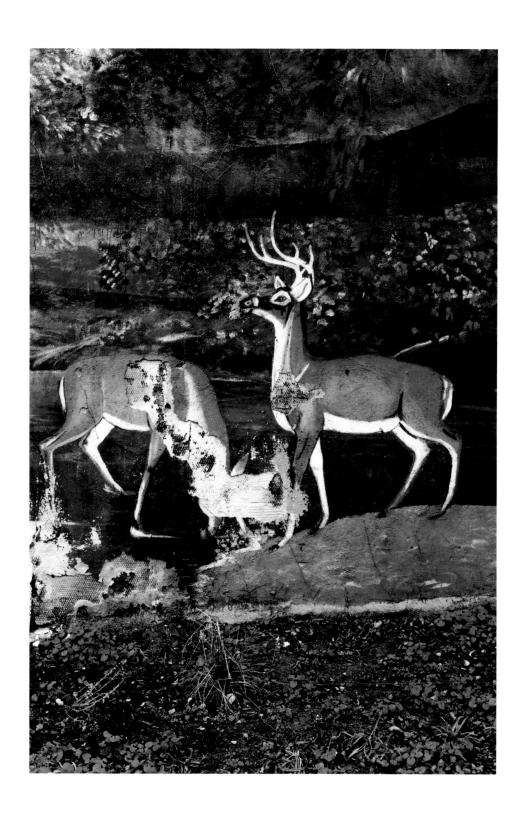

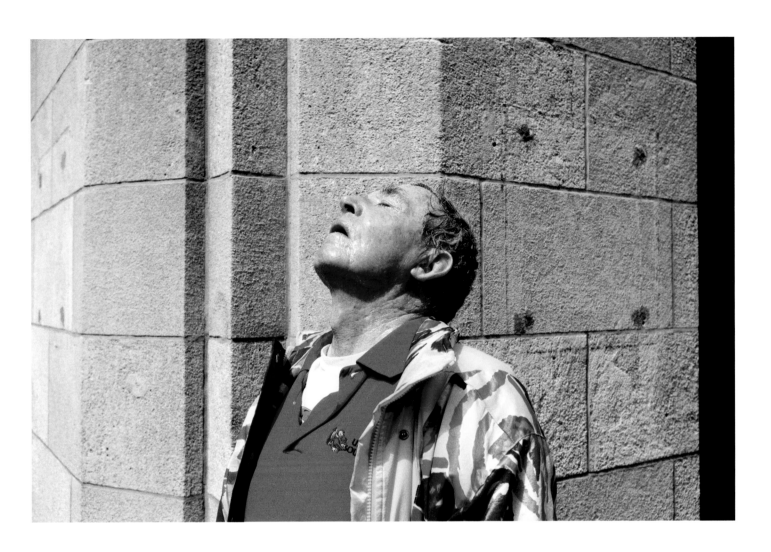

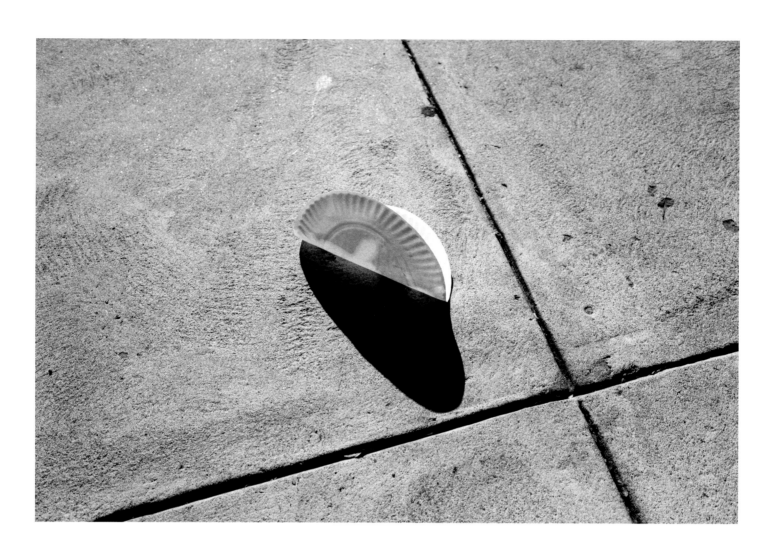

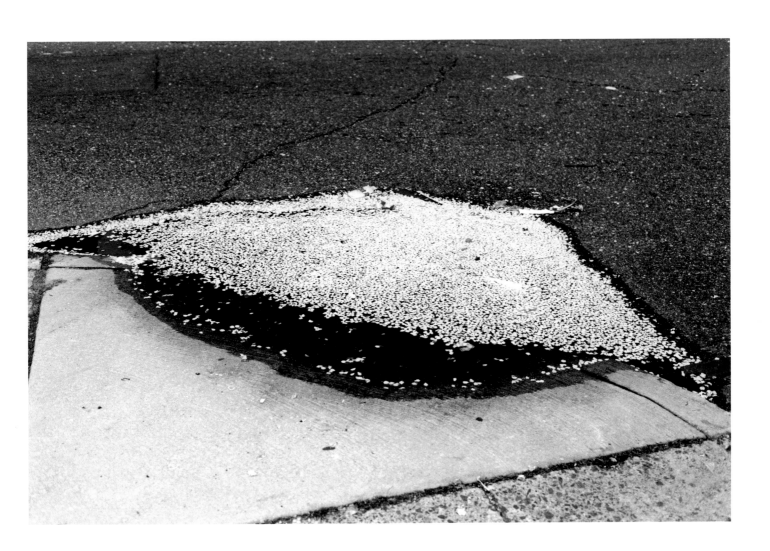

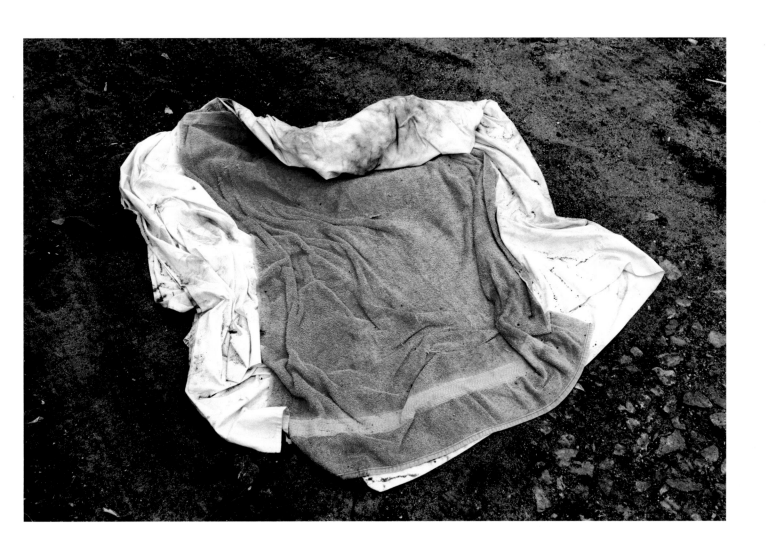

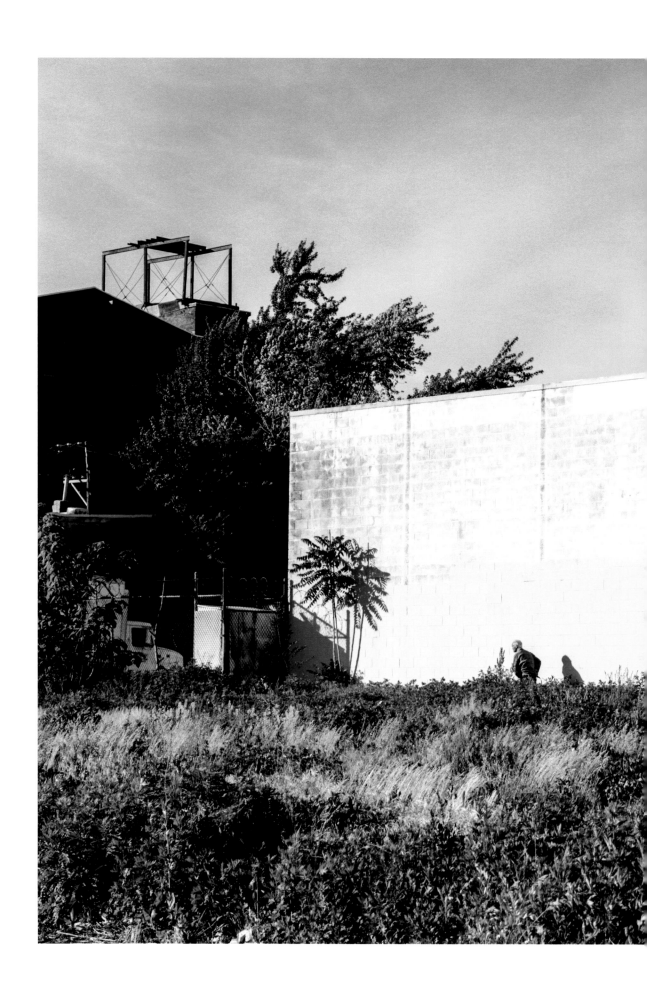

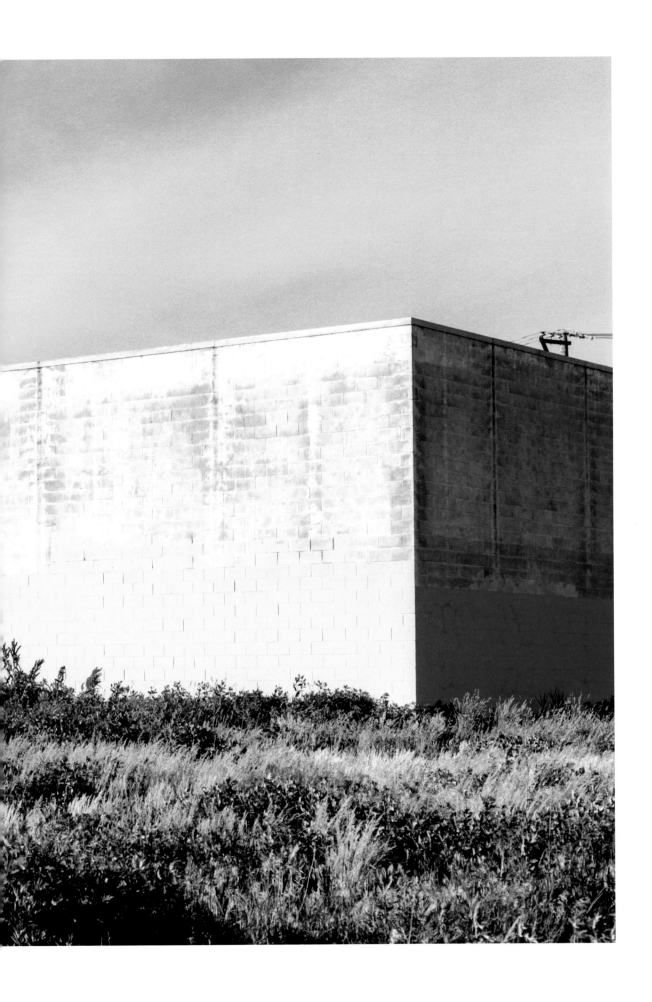

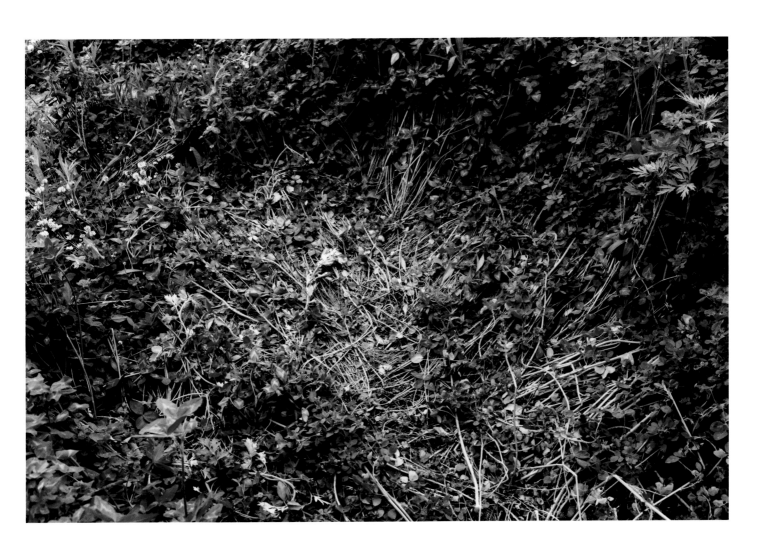

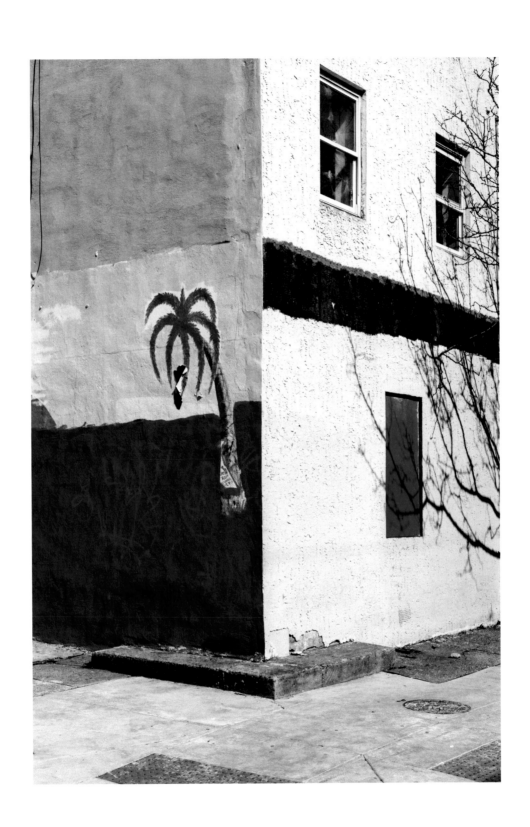

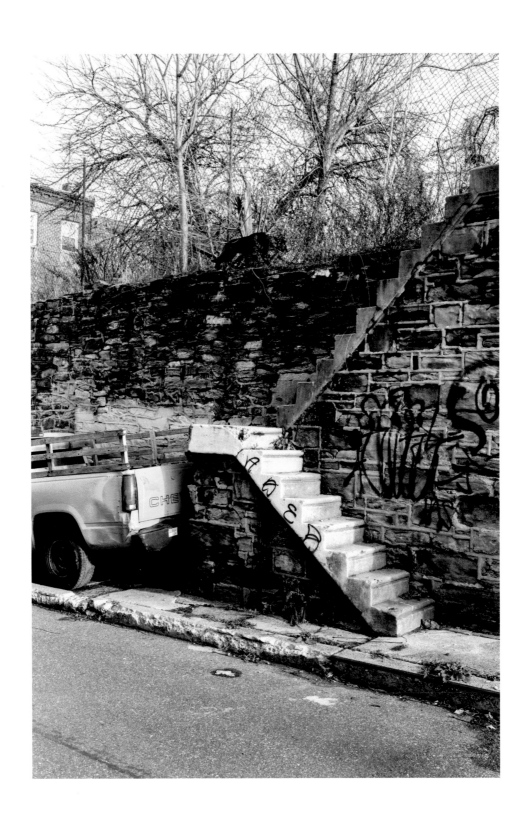

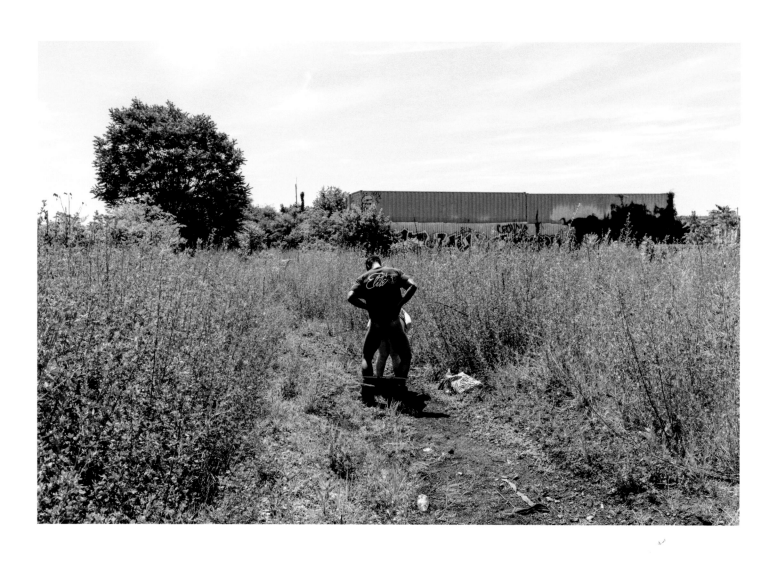

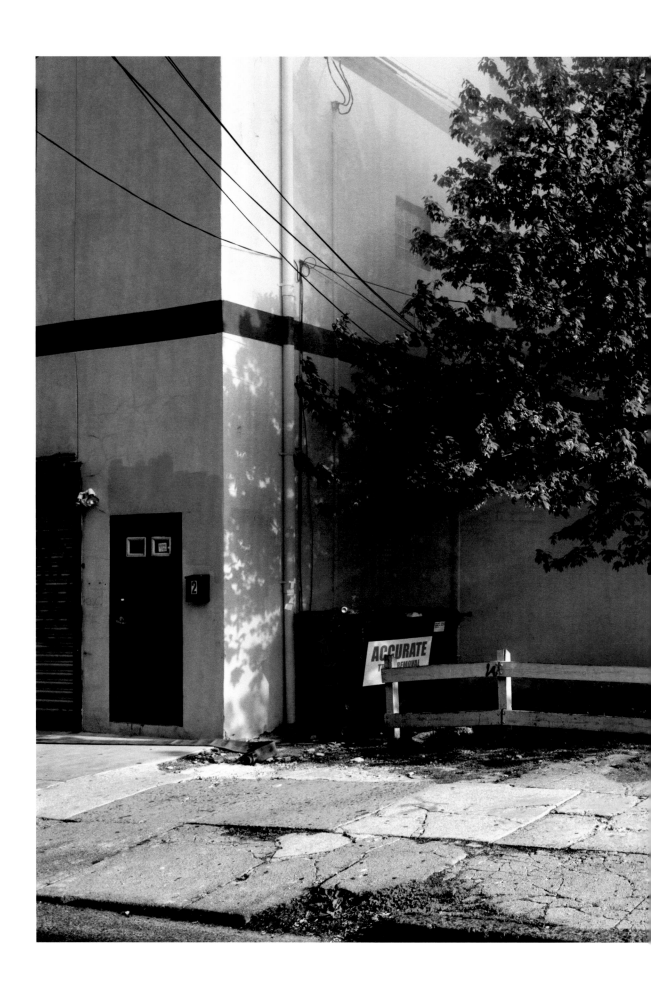

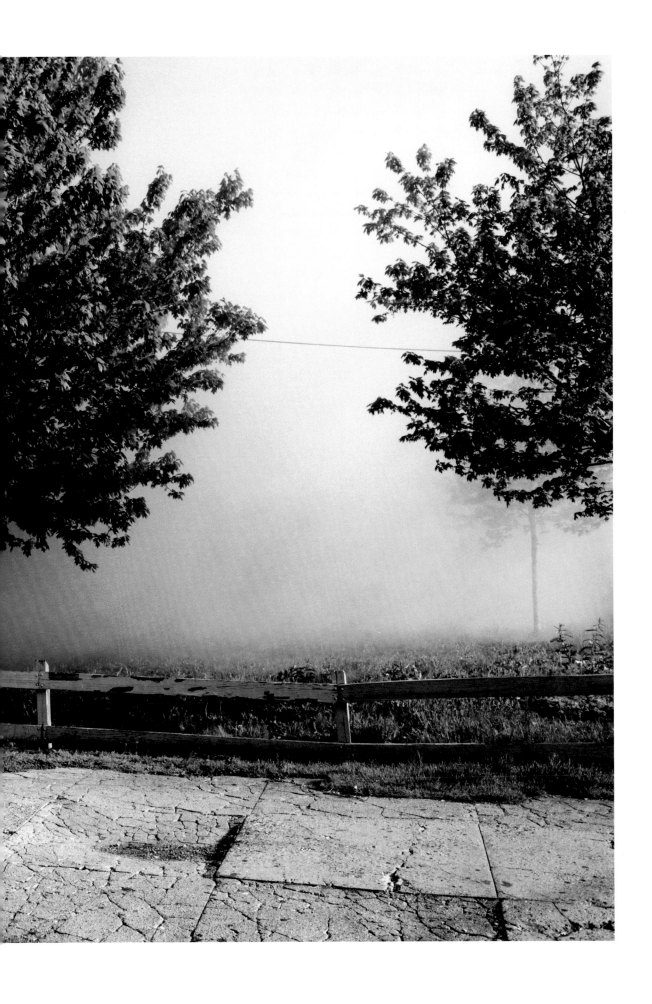

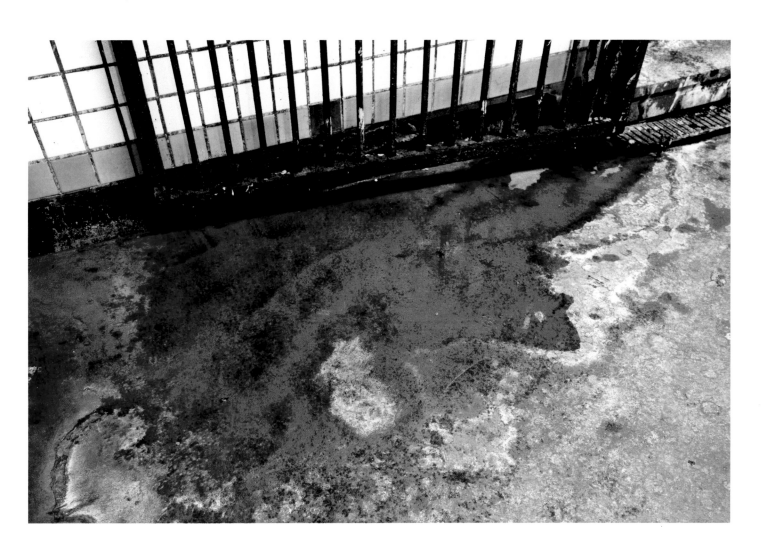

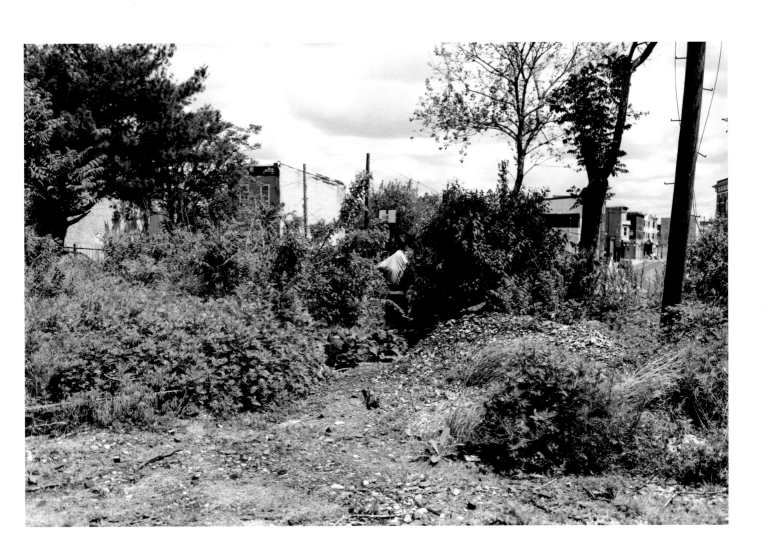

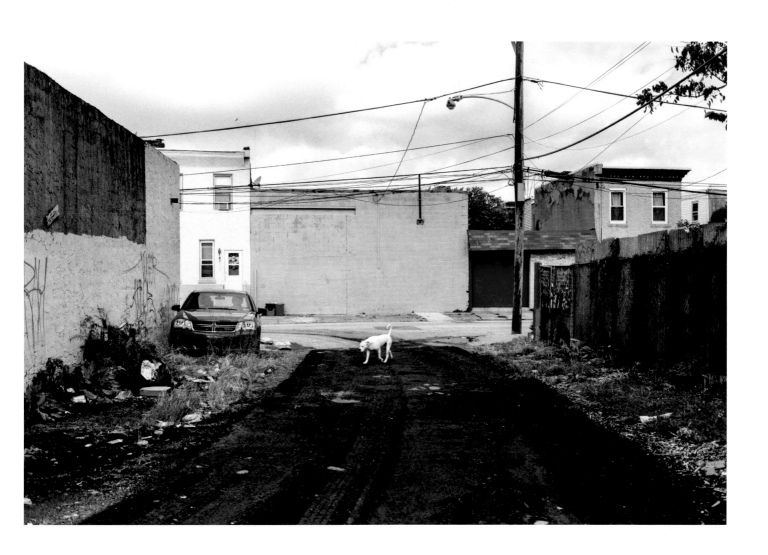

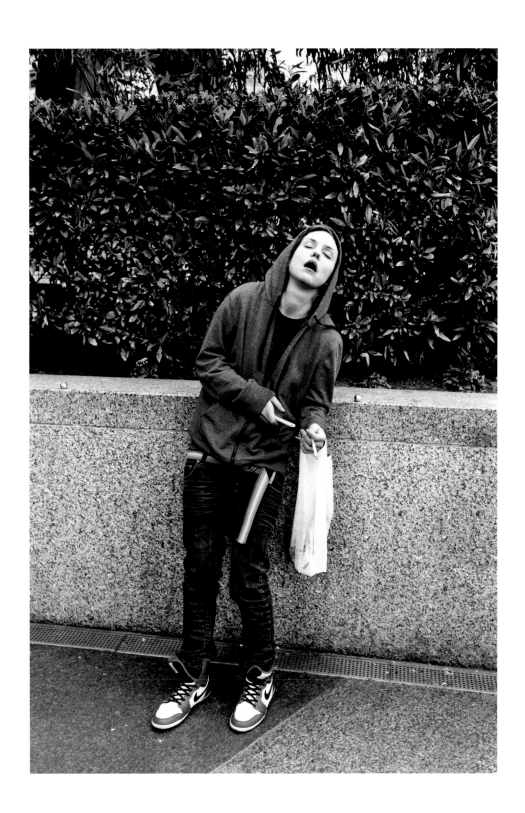

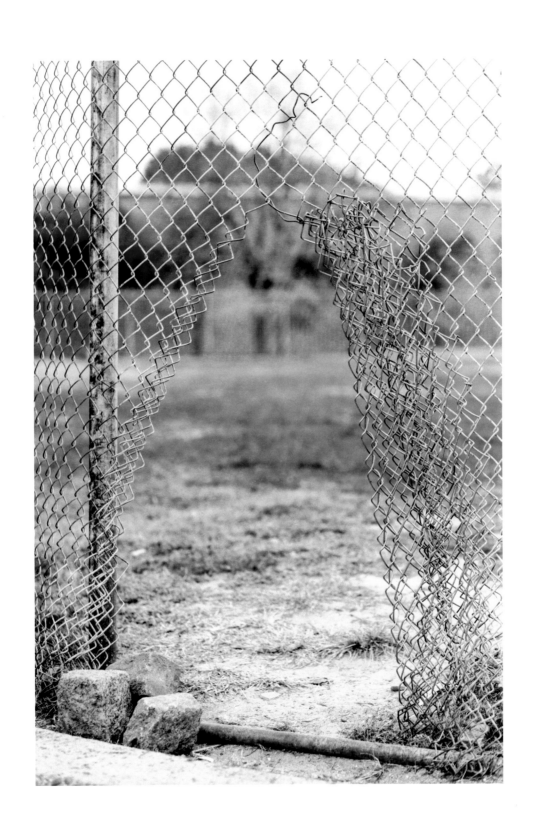

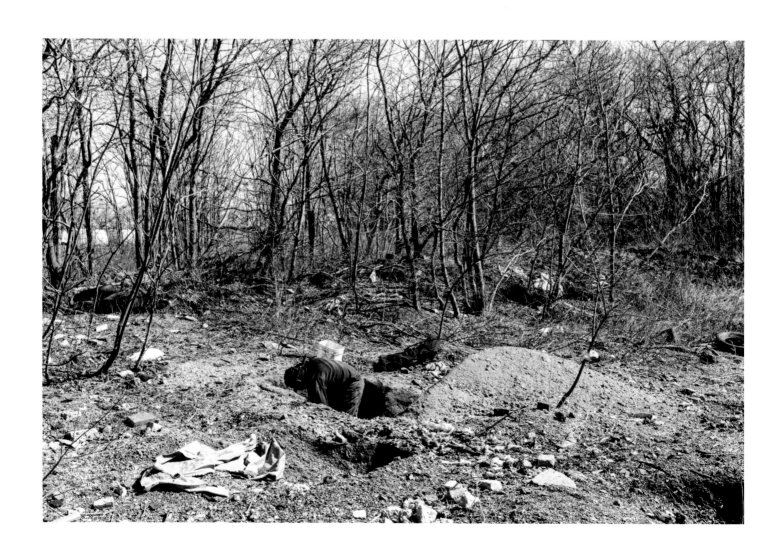

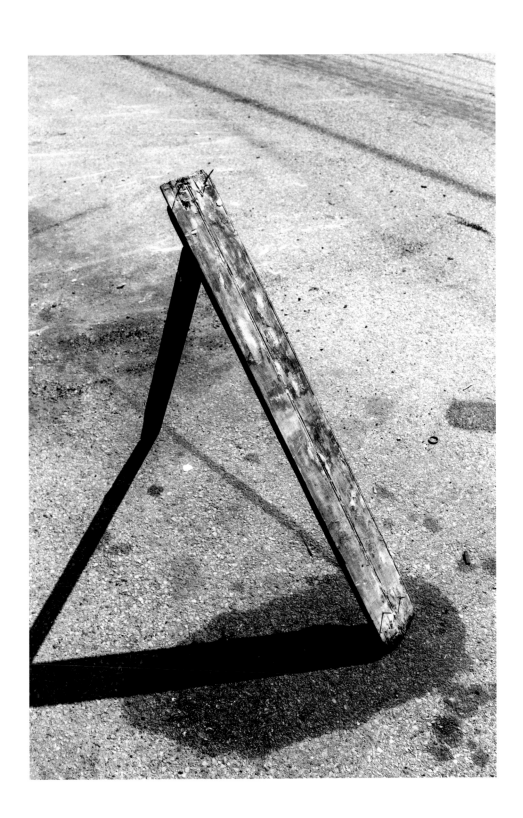

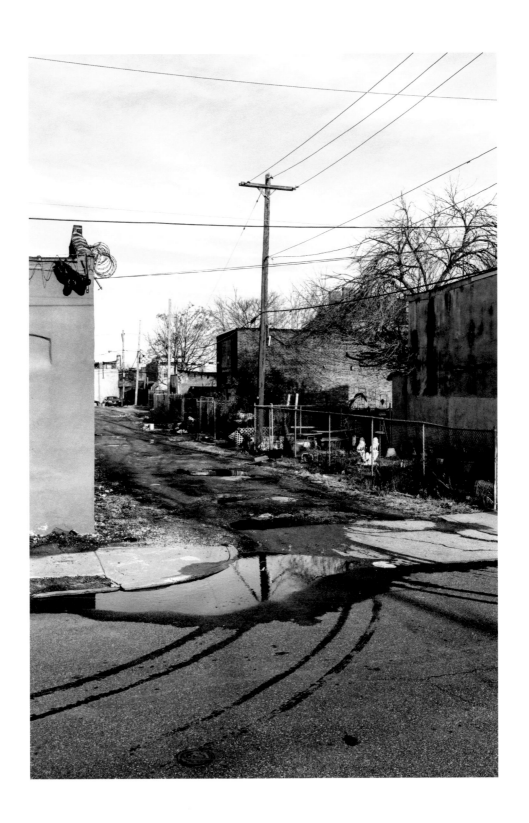

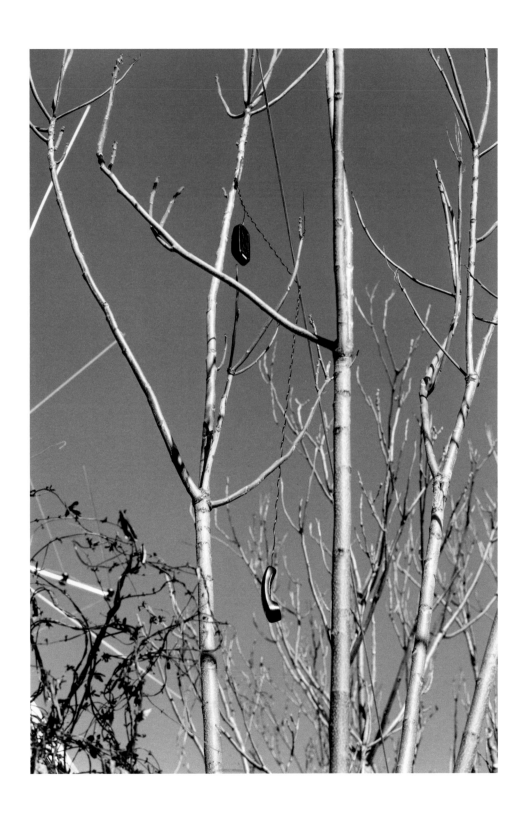

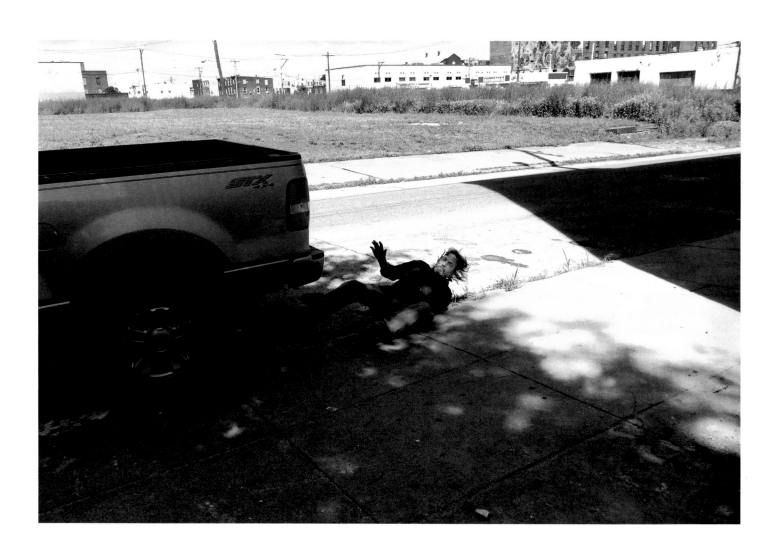

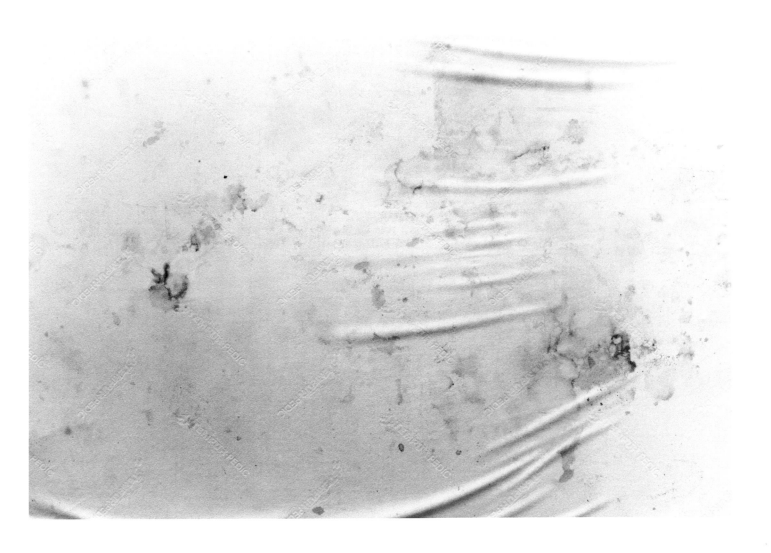

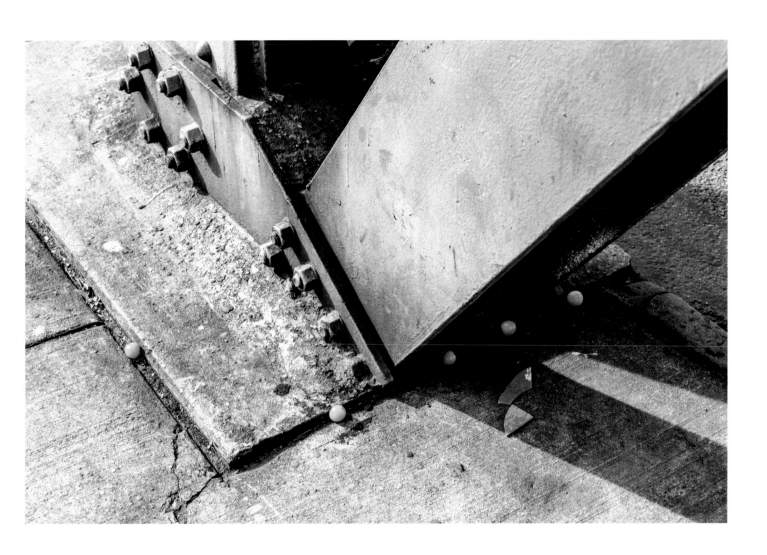

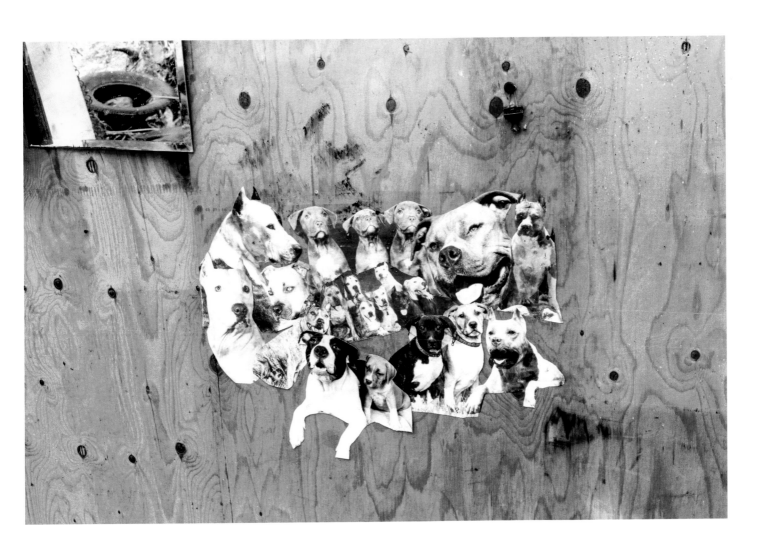

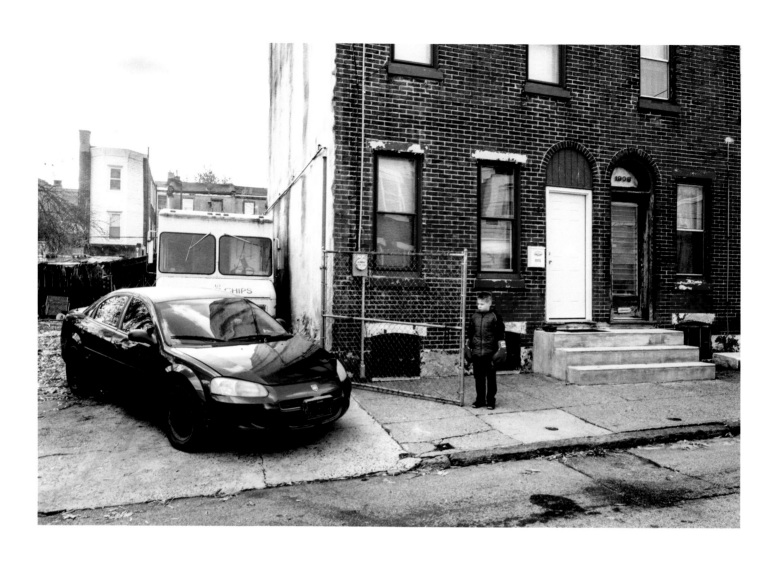

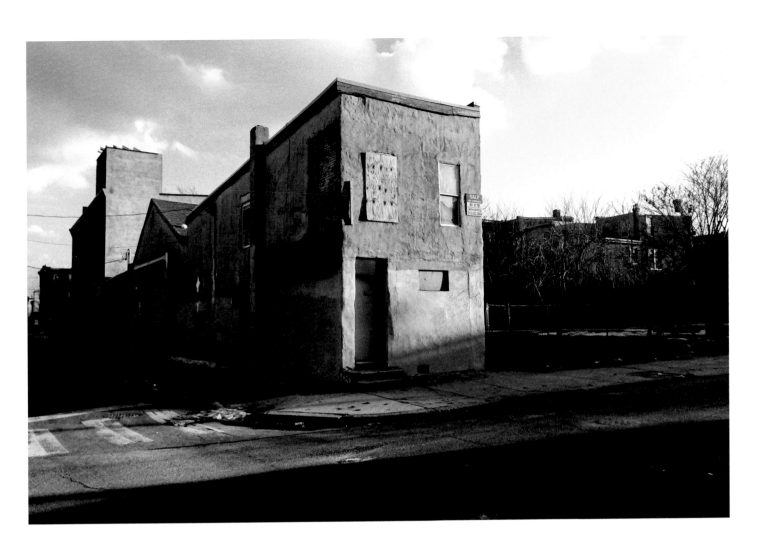

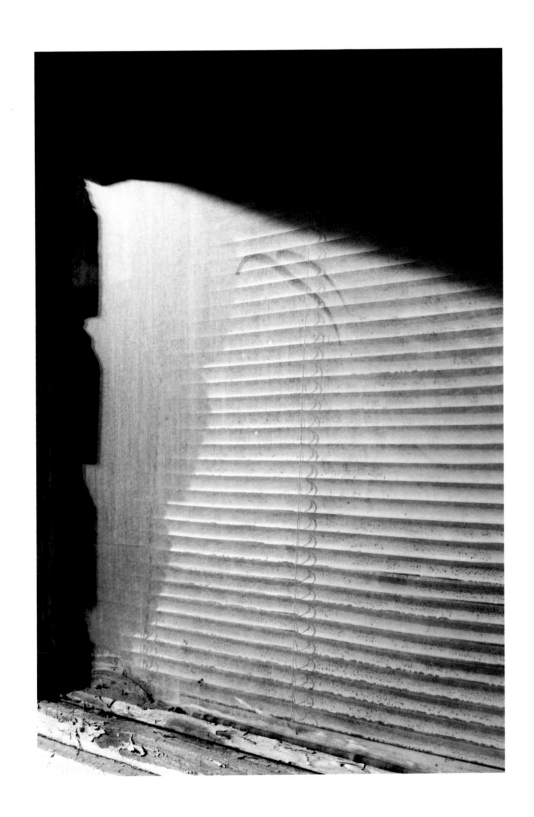

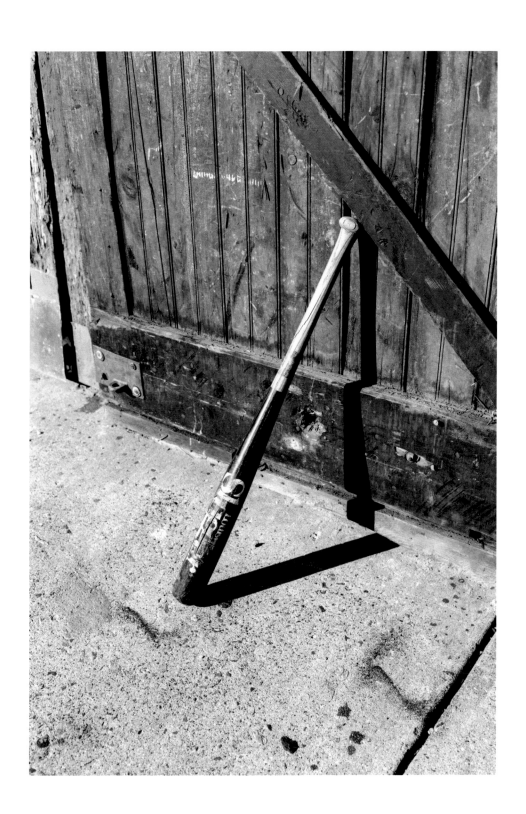

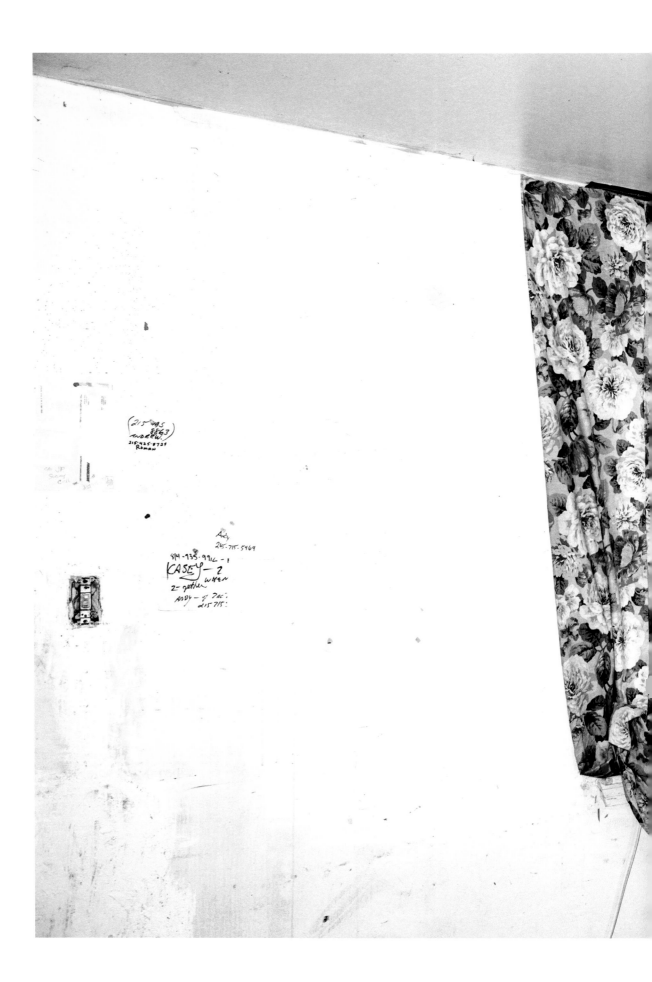

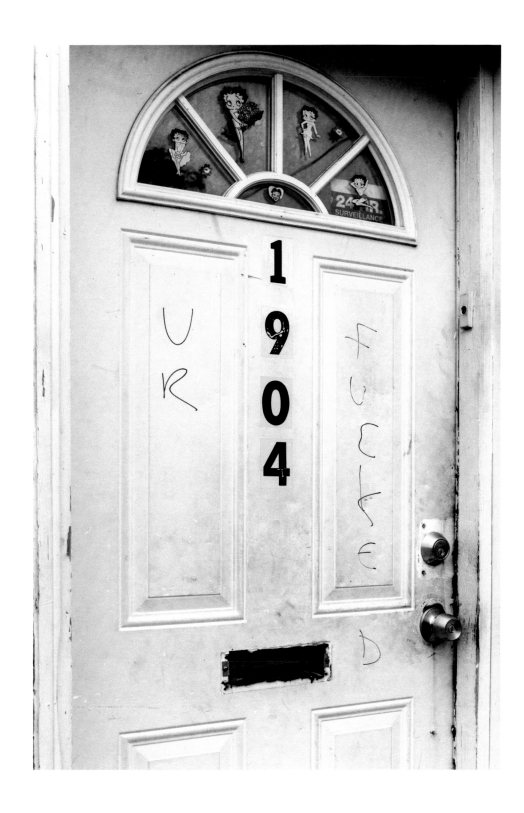

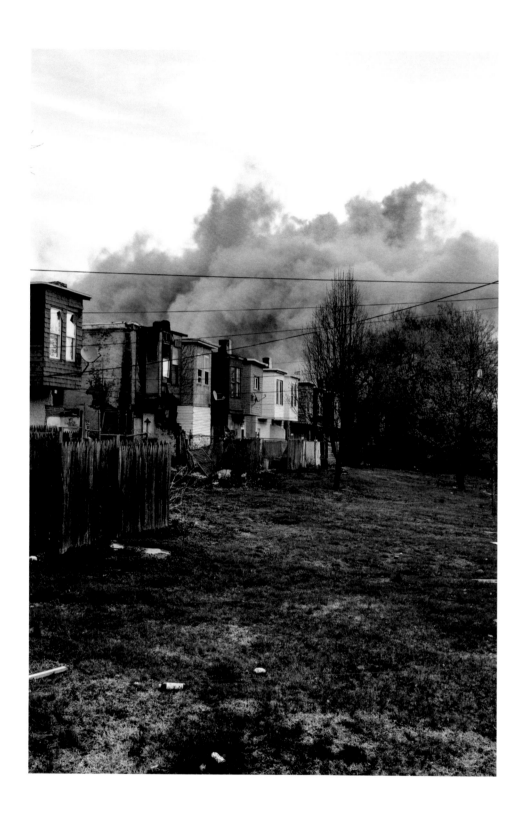

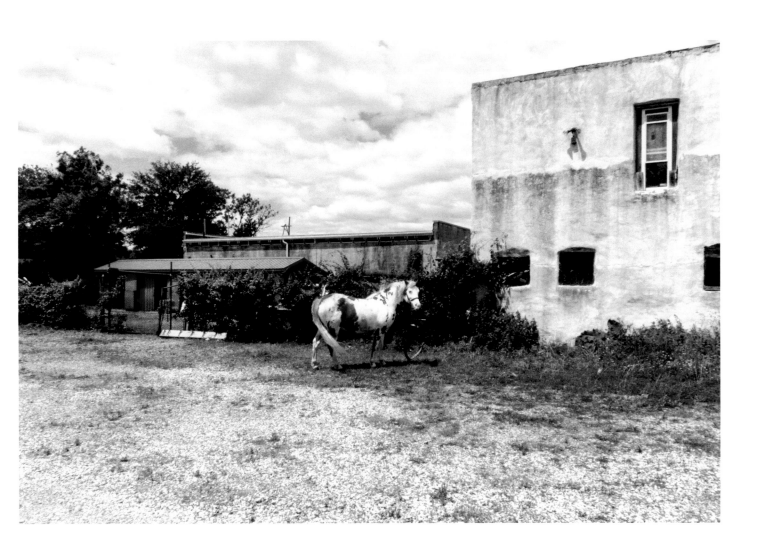

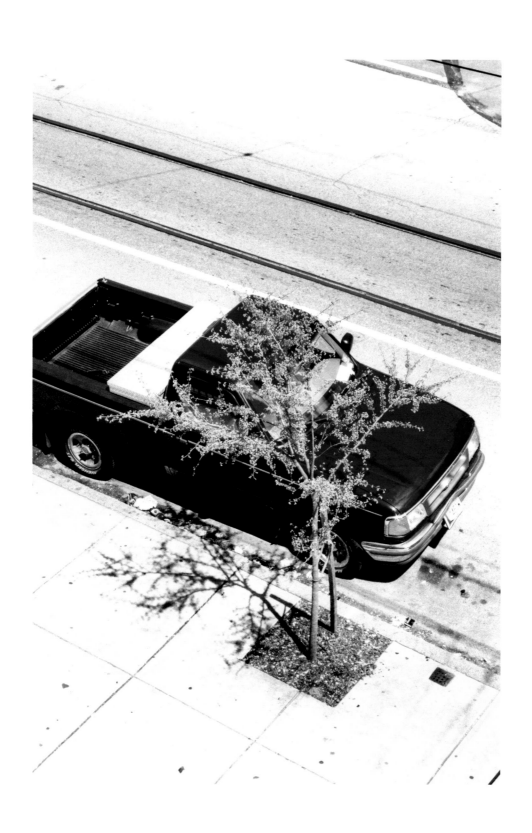

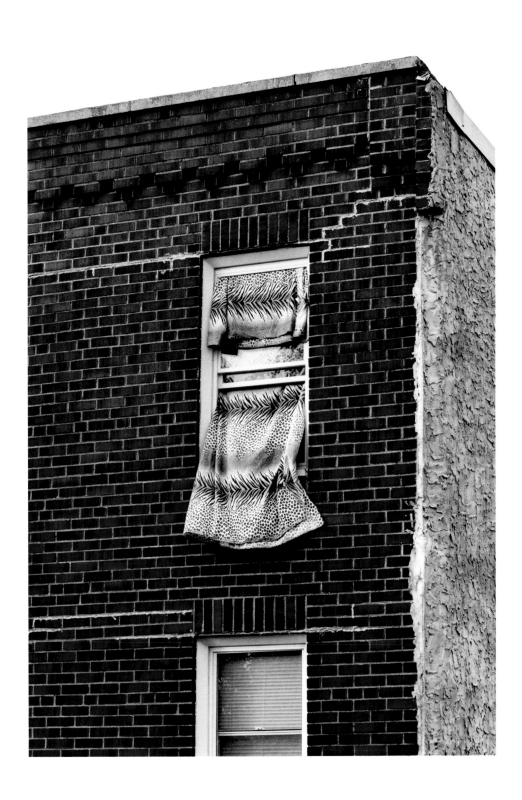

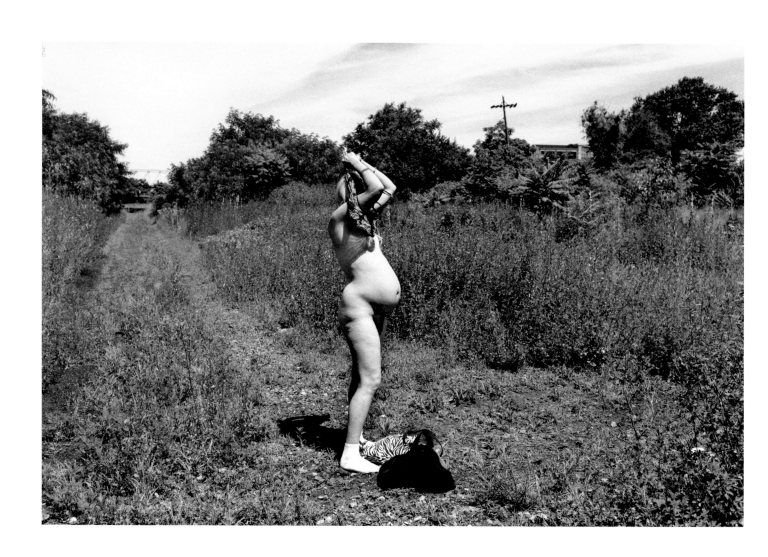

My neighbor's kitchen looks onto the field with the high grass by the blue and white building off Boston Street. When he squints through his window he says it looks like the sky goes on forever.

They found an overdosed man's body in the field with the high grass. Rumor is when they discovered him, the needle was still in his arm and he was clutching rosaries. We'd been trying to get that high grass mowed for at least a month but bureaucracy takes time.

I stumbled upon a prostitute giving a man a blowjob in the field with the high grass. He told me he was gonna whoop my ass but I reminded him his dick was out.

One New Year's Eve, I watched a man fire an assault rifle into the air while he stood in the field with the high grass. He left for a little bit but later came back with more ammo.

A makeshift camp popped up in the field with the high grass. The police never saw it because they never got out of their car when they drove past. One evening, a neighbor and I watched as the whole camp went up in flames. He turned to me and said, "I guess that's the best way that could have ended."

A fence now surrounds the field with the high grass by the blue and white building off Boston Street. Inside it, there are dump trucks and backhoes. It's going to be luxury housing soon, I'm sure.

9 781910 401194

GOST

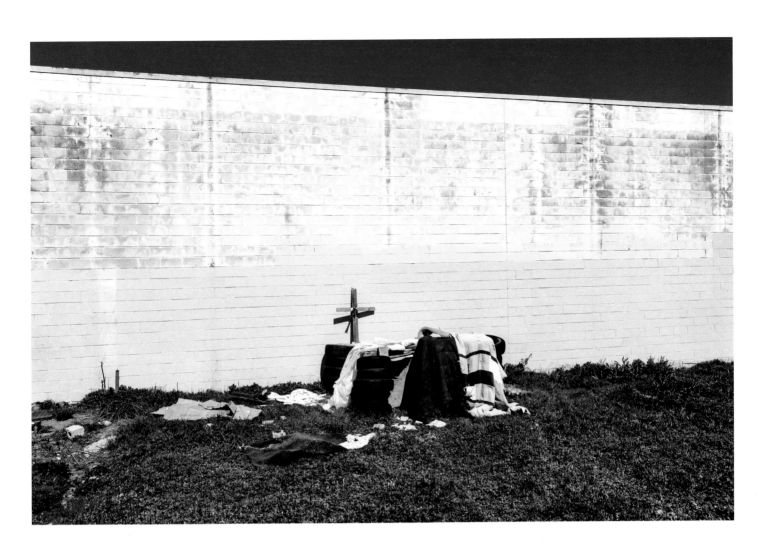

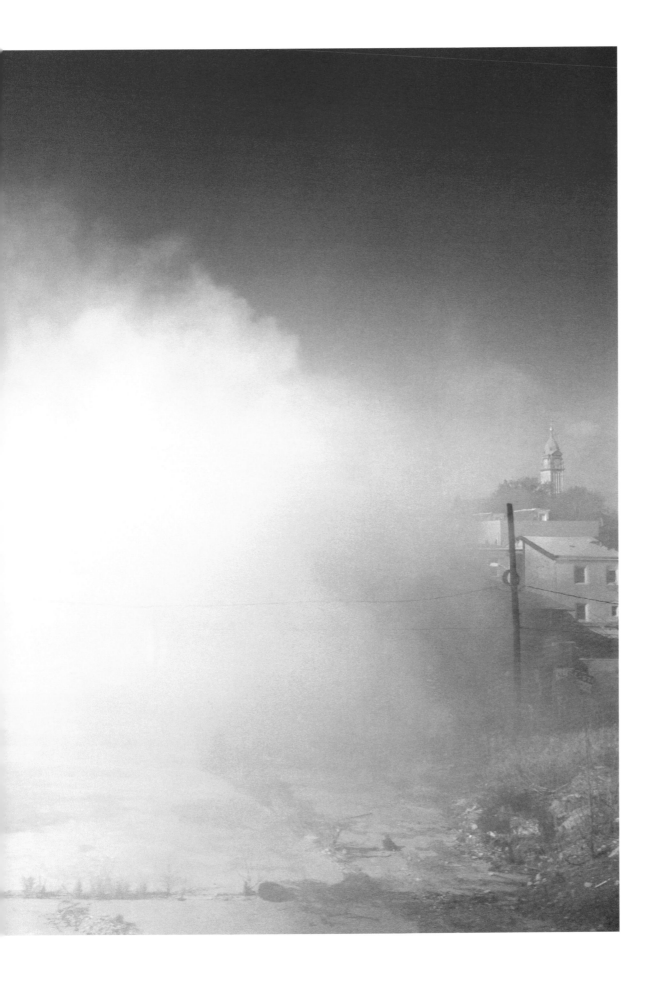

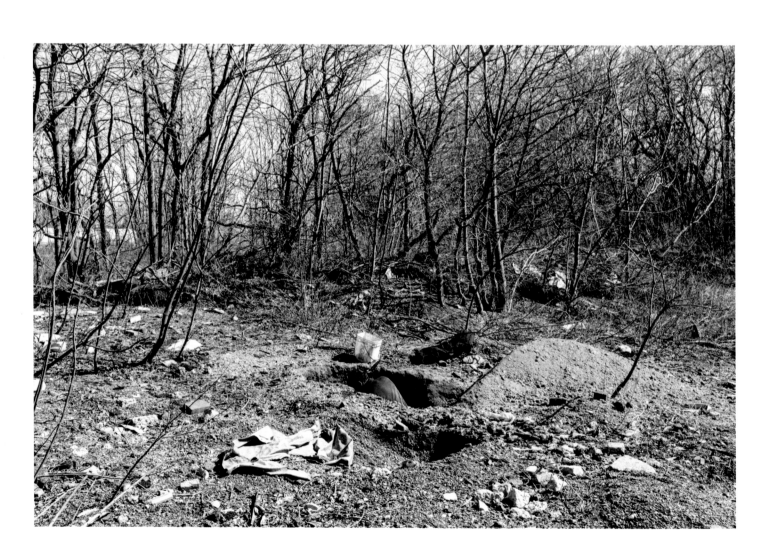

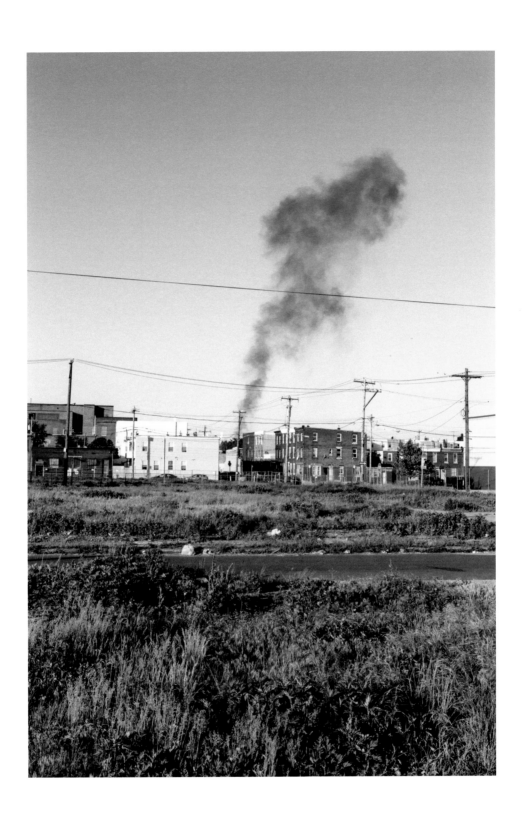

Thank you to my creative community, without you this
work would not have been possible: Stephanie Bursese,
Tim Carpenter, Nelson Chan, Jenny Drumgoole,
Dominic Episcopo, Christopher Gianunzio, Taylor
Galloway, Caroline Gore, Ian Kline, Jay Muhlin, Anna
Neighbor, Steven B. Smith, Chad States, Keith Yahrling,
and my colleagues at the University of the Arts.

Thank you to those who made generous contributions
to the project: Ryan Hancock & Melanie Bilenker,
Larry Reichlin, Christina & Adam Schoon, Vincent
Schiavone, Max Tuttleman, The Hamilton Family
Foundation, and the University of the Arts
President's Fund for Excellence.

A very special thank you to Joel Evey for his guidance,
initial layout and design. Thank you to Niki Ververelli,
my family, and my neighbors for creating a space full
of love and support. Also, thank you to Stuart Smith
and everyone at GOST for believing in the project,
helping me break my own rules, and for the tremendous
amount of work they did to bring this book to print.
And, of course thank you to Anne, without whom
I surely wouldn't be alive.

Philadelphia, you mean everything to me.

First published in 2018 by
GOST Books
8a West Smithfield
London
EC1A 9JR
info@gostbooks.com
gostbooks.com

© GOST Books
Images © Jordan Baumgarten
Edited and designed by GOST:
Katie Clifford, Allon Kaye, Eleanor Macnair,
Claudia Paladini, Ana Rocha, Justine Schuster

Printed in Italy by EBS

British Library cataloguing-in-publication data.
A catalogue record of this book is available from
the British Library.

ISBN 978-1-910401-19-4

GOST